Mummies

By Stephen Rickard

Published in 2026 by
Norwood House Press
2544 Clinton Street
Buffalo, NY 14224

Printed in the United States of America

Library of Congress Cataloging-in-Publication Data:
Names: Rickard, Stephen, 1957-, author. | Atkins, Jill (Children's author). | Cain, Martyn, illustrator.
Title: Mummies / by Stephen Rickard. Zak's gift / written by Jill Atkins, illustrated by Martyn Cain.
Description: Buffalo, NY : Norwood House Press, 2026. | Series: Phonics all-stars: phase 5c
Identifiers: ISBN 9781978578470 (pbk.) | ISBN 9781978578487 (library bound) | ISBN 9781978578494 (ebook)
Subjects: LCSH: Reading–Phonetic method–Juvenile literature. | English language–Phonetics–Juvenile literature. | Mummies–Juvenile literature. | Sheep–Juvenile fiction.
Classification: LCC LB1573.3 R534 2026 | DDC 372.465–dc23

CPSIA compliance information: Batch #CW26NHP: For further information contact Norwood House Press at 1-800-237-9932.

What is a mummy?

A mummy is a dead human or animal that has been dried out and kept in a box or a coffin.

ody was treated
to protect the soft
e body, such as the
e brain.

rts of the body
n jars like this one.

Sometimes, a mummy is made by people.

This happened long ago in Egypt, when important people were made into mummies after they died.

The mask of a mummy from Egypt.

Mummies can happen in nature too.

When a creature dies, it may turn into a mummy if the surroundings are very cold and dry.

This frog has turned into a mummy.

Long ago in Egypt, people turned important kings and queens into mummies. We think that the first mummies in Egypt were made over 5,000 years ago.

They bound the mummies in cloth, which was tightly stretched over the body, and then put them in stone or wooden coffins.

They made mummies from the bodies of cats, crocodiles, and even apes too.

In Egypt, people thought that their kings and queens lived on after death, in the **afterlife**.

These important people needed their bodies in the afterlife, so huge pyramids were constructed to keep the bodies of the kings and queens safe.

In Egypt, the pyramids are now an imposing feature in the landscape.

The people of Egypt thought that in the afterlife their kings and queens needed things like gold, gems, chairs, goblets, and even food.

The kings and queens might be hungry when they reached the afterlife.

So they placed these goods in the pyramids, next to the coffins.

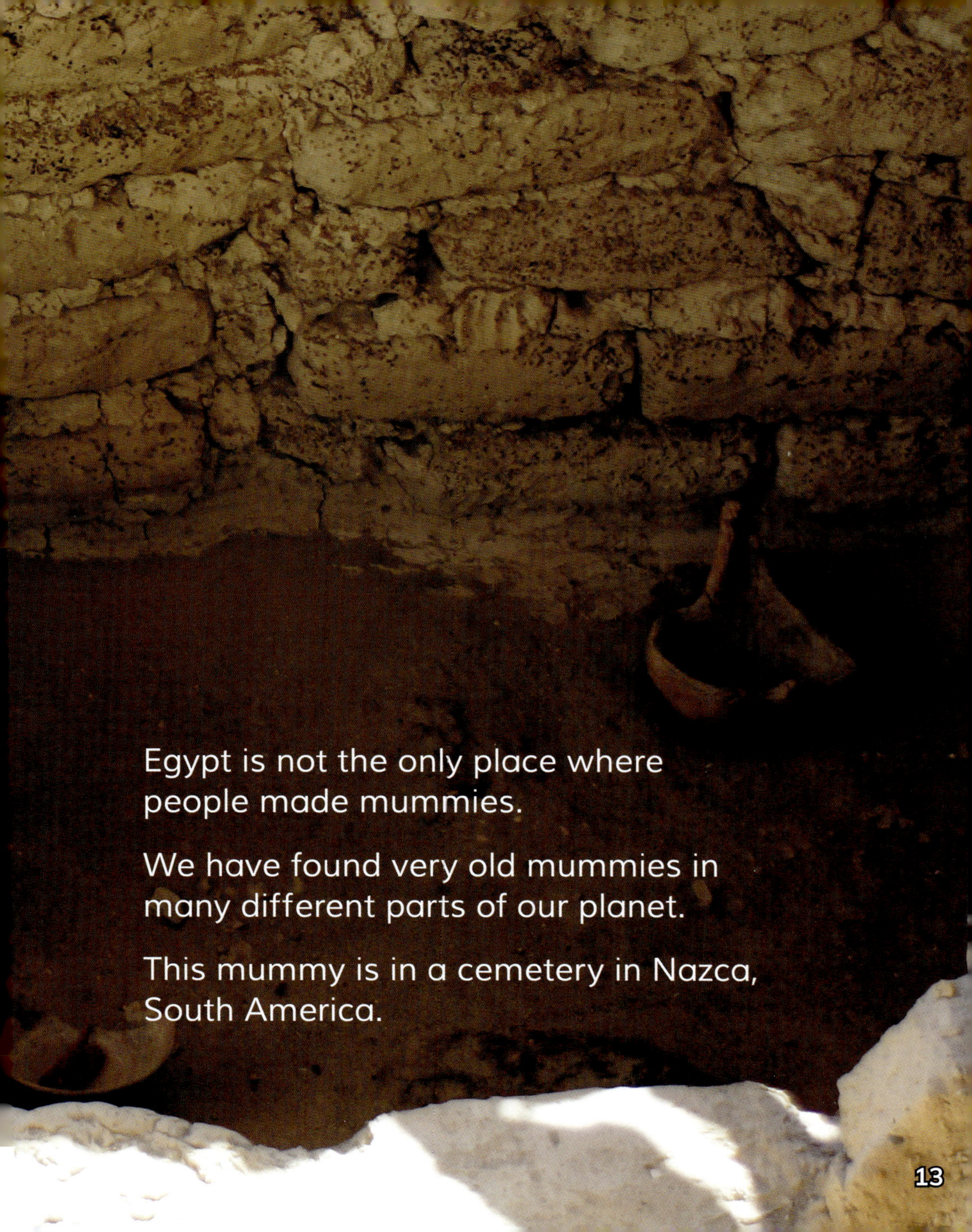

Egypt is not the only place where people made mummies.

We have found very old mummies in many different parts of our planet.

This mummy is in a cemetery in Nazca, South America.

Over seventy years ago, in Denmark, some people found the body of a man in a peat bog.

They thought the man had only just died, but in fact the body had been there for over 2,400 years.

The bog had turned his body into a mummy.

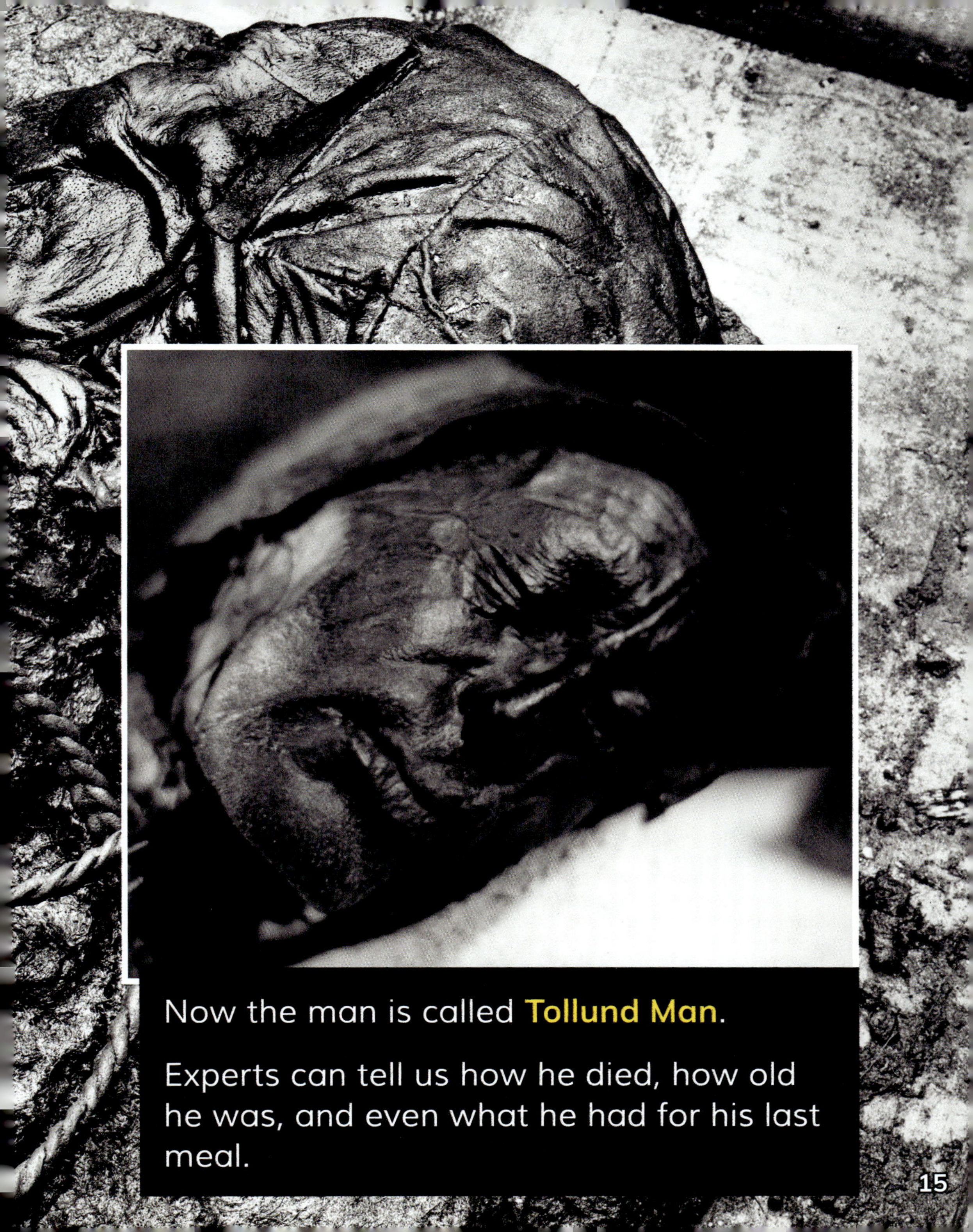

Now the man is called **Tollund Man**.

Experts can tell us how he died, how old he was, and even what he had for his last meal.

Some people think it is bad luck to open a mummy's coffin.

Some people even think that mummies can come back to life.

Really?

Zak's Gift

Written by
Jill Atkins

Illustrated by
Martyn Cain

Zak and his friends charged through the woods, looking for the best tree to climb.

It was difficult keeping up with Danny and Joe, and when they reached the tree, Zak was out of breath.

Zak glanced at the badger hole beneath the tree, then he began to climb.

At last, Zak was sitting high in the tree. He could see sheep in the field below.

This was so relaxing, away from the problems of school.

Joe and Danny were in the top class at school. They were really brainy – teachers said they were "gifted." They were good at sports too.

Zak found it hard at school. He just wasn't any good at sitting in class, studying, and doing exams.

Sometimes Joe and Danny being so good made Zak feel bad.

Later on, Danny said, "Let's go exploring."

Zak and Joe gave a thumbs-up!

They dashed over a bridge and ran alongside a hedge, until they reached a gate.

As they climbed over the gate, Zak whispered.

"We mustn't frighten the sheep. They're all pregnant."

"What? How can you tell?" asked Danny.

"Seen it on TV," said Zak. "And it's springtime."

As they skirted around the edge of the field, Zak suddenly stopped.

“That sheep,” he said, pointing. “She’s got a problem.” He edged a bit nearer.

"She needs help," he said. "We have to tell the farmer."

He could see the farm just a few fields away.

Danny nudged Joe. "You go," he said.

"Why don't you both go?" said Zak. "You're both fast runners, aren't you?"

The boys raced away.

Zak hoped that the sheep would feel better with him there.

Then it bleated loudly. Was a lamb about to be born?

Zak steadied his nerves as he pulled the tiny feet that had appeared.

It wasn't easy, but Zak just seemed to feel it was the right thing to do.

At last, Zak fell back. There it was. A tiny newborn lamb!

He grabbed some straw and rubbed the body, then he edged the lamb nearer to its mom. She began to lick it clean.

Now Zak could hear the quad bike approaching.

The farmer jumped off the bike and noticed the lamb.

"Did you deliver this lamb?" she asked.

Zak nodded.

"Excellent!" she said.

Then Zak noticed the sheep.

“I think there’s a second lamb,” he said.

A few moments later, there were twin lambs. Zak had delivered them both!

"Would you like to help with the lambing?" the farmer asked, as they lifted the sheep and lambs onto the trailer. "You're a star!"

Zak beamed. "Can I?"

It felt so good to be helping animals like this – and he'd never been called a star in his life.

Had Zak found his gift?